There are 72 Hours in a Day

There are 72 Hours in a Day

USING EFFICIENCY TO BETTER ENJOY EVERY PART OF YOUR LIFE

Dr. Jeffrey E. Sterling

ISBN: 154087205X
ISBN 13: 9781540872050
Library of Congress Control Number: 2016920375
CreateSpace Independent Publishing Platform
North Charleston, South Carolina

Contents

Introduction

Whether or not you believe the notion that we only use 5 percent of our brainpower, perhaps that consideration should apply to our level of efficiency. Each of us intuitively knows that we could achieve greater productivity than we typically do.

I'm an emergency physician. Being able to competently take care of ten to fifteen patients at a time is part of the job description. When done well, that job requires clinical and technical competence. Furthermore, the job requires that we make each patient feel as if he or she is the center of our universe. We must be competent and efficient at many things in order to make the process flow seamlessly. One should always wonder how anyone in a busy emergency department gets the care they need! Well, we wonder, and there is indeed a method to what may appear to be madness!

I'm also a health-care consultant. The job description is typically, "Fix it; fix it fast; and fix it so it lasts." This requires prompt assessment, determination of problems and multiple possible solutions, incorporation of solutions within the culture of the organization, implementation of the plan, staff education, and transfer of ownership of the solution to the stakeholders. It can be a rather intense process.

I'm also a business owner, a public-health professional, the president of one of my college's alumni associations, and I sit on corporate boards. I write a daily blog on public health and matters of health, and I'm an author. Most importantly, I'm a husband and a father of young children. I take over one hundred flights annually, play one hundred rounds of golf per year, and love to exercise. Still, I almost always have more time on my hands than my friends, and I always seem to find myself waiting for others to catch up to me.

I used to think it would be cool if I could be the guy who was able to function on three hours of sleep. I thought that would be the ultimate indicator of being incredibly productive. I'm really glad I learned that it's not the time spent that matters. What's more important is the ability to produce the desired outcome. Getting to this point required learning to be organized and efficient.

People always ask me why I seem so accessible given how busy I am. Simply put, I have discovered the value of seconds. Once you reach a certain level of efficiency, you can accomplish an increasing amount in an incrementally lesser amount of time.

Regarding efficiency, I like to think there are seventy-two hours in a day, and I have a lot of fun executing that concept. I also love the notion of five-minute efficiency—you'll see what I mean by that later. Between these last two considerations, I'm now able to complete tasks in much less time than it may have in the past, while performing at the same, if not a higher, level of performance.

I know what you're thinking. "That sounds crazy!" "How can I get it all in?" "It's too stressful." "There's work, family, and friends; I never have enough time." "I'm too busy to exercise. I grab fast food on the run. I'm up all night catching up on work. I never see my family. I can't do any more than I'm already doing!" "Do you sleep?"

This book isn't about being maniacally active. It's about understanding and appreciating the various levels of efficiency. It's about applying those levels to your life in a way that helps you produce the quality of life versus work balance that keeps you happy and fulfilled. This book will give you a different way of thinking about your activities and will give you the tools you need to become better organized, more efficient, and more productive. Just maybe, it will also show you how to better enjoy the work you do.

If you follow the principles outlined in this book, you will place yourself on a path to discovering ever-increasing levels of efficiency. It's all about working smarter, not harder. The goal is seventy-two hours of productivity, not seventy-two hours of work. In fact, I'm out to prove to you that the number of hours in a day actually has very little to do with your level of productivity! If you prove me right, imagine the extra amount of time you'll have at your disposal. Imagine all that you could accomplish and the effect you could have. Imagine the freedom to spend additional time with your friends, family, and loved ones. Whatever level of efficiency you achieve, don't forget to have fun with it. Enjoy the journey.

SECTION I

Learning Efficiency

This is not a book of tips. It's a book of principles. Just as, over the long run, it's better to teach you how to fish than to simply give you a fish, this book seeks to instill a philosophy of living efficiently. Once you learn these principles and incorporate them into your life, you will become so efficient that you will find yourself taking advantage of opportunities that you previously hadn't even known existed.

CHAPTER 1

Your Approach to Productivity
Could Be Better

Most people are trying to be productive, although that often doesn't appear to be the case. Many of us seem to approach tasks as if we just want to finish them and be done with it. Achieving the highest levels of productivity involves embracing tasks and relishing the opportunities they provide us with. You've heard people ask, "What's the best way to eat an elephant?" If your answer is "One bite at a time," you're only partially right. You've heard people ask, "What's the best way to take a journey of a thousand steps?" If your answer is "One step at a time," you're only partially right. I would suggest the better answer to both questions is "With a plan!" We'll discuss the planning process later on.

Look around at your colleagues at work and play. Most of us take a task and look at the amount of time we have allotted for the task. We then take as much time as we have available to complete the task. Too often, we wait until the last minute, rush to complete the task, and end up missing deadlines.

In medical school, I was often frustrated by my study habits. If I had a week before a test, I would spend every available second studying. As I walked into the exam hall, I would still be studying. My roommate would study for a while and then move on to something else—something more enjoyable than studying. It wasn't that I needed the extra time to learn the material; it was just that I was worried that if I didn't study that much, I wouldn't do my best. Interestingly, my roommate and I would always end up with virtually the same results.

Lesson learned: *productivity involves compressing time.*

People ask me all the time to help them be more productive. I typically respond by asking them what their approach is to being productive. In most cases, people identify tasks and deadlines, and they figure they'll get around to it when they have the time or feel motivated to work. We see this in people's work efforts, their exercise habits, and their home lives. Wouldn't you rather get to the items on your personal and professional bucket lists sooner? Why not live and accomplish on the fly? You can if you discover the efficiencies life has to offer!

An additional problem with our quest for productivity is our notion of what represents quality. In a phrase, many of us approach tasks and make "perfection the enemy of good." Productivity seeks a "good enough" measure of success; of course, "good enough" can and should represent a very high standard of excellence, but that's not the point of productivity. We lose productivity when we assign increasing amounts of time to a project and receive decreasing returns on incremental quality produced. Even scientists have accepted this notion, such that in research studies, a 5 percent margin of error is statistically significant enough to be viewed as definitive and acceptable.

Have you ever learned about the political process of passing a bill? Have you ever heard that many legislators don't even read the bills they pass? Without making any value judgments on the process, there's actually a reason for that, and it's based on productivity. Besides the fact that politicians have staffers who review bills and distill the fine points for consumption, there is value in simply getting bills passed.

More importantly, there is something to be said about simply passing bills based on good concepts. Passing a bill is not etching something in stone but is typically defining the parameters of a policy goal. As an example, think about how many revisions Social Security and Medicare have gone through since their initial approval. Time spent attempting to craft a perfect bill is time wasted, as future legislators will inevitably make adjustments based on the evolving needs of the general public. Looking at the legislative process from a productivity standpoint, politicians identify the key components of success and negotiate the rest. This is what defines progress. Productivity is reproducing that process as frequently as is practical.

To be clear: I'm not at all advocating sloppiness in your work. That wouldn't be productive. Having to go back and revise your efforts is actually counterproductive. That said, I am suggesting that you realize there are different levels to success. Find the balance between quality and quantity of output in all your endeavors. Just as engineers have baseline specifications that define quality and don't require every shipment to be absolutely constructed to perfection, you should learn to perform at a high enough level that your productivity doesn't get stifled.

CHAPTER 2

Getting to Outcomes

Most of what we do is a means to an end. We have a job to do. We have an outcome to reach. The eternal challenge of our work is figuring out how to perform the job as efficiently and effectively as possible. I remember learning one relevant lesson about this as a graduate student at Harvard. The professor was discussing research. The idea was simple: the best research is done as if you've written the paper first and then conducted the research to determine if your hypothesis was correct.

Over twenty years later, this nugget of wisdom has permeated virtually every aspect of my life.

- As a physician, I develop a list of probable causes for a patient's symptoms (called the differential diagnosis). I then ask the patient questions, perform a physical examination, and order tests to determine the probability of these considerations.
- As a consultant, I create project plans and implementation matrices at the beginning of every project that take the client step by step through the process, demonstrating how the outcome of interest will be obtained.
- As a husband, I identify typical obstacles that lead away from a healthy, happy marriage and toward divorce. I then determine how to avoid them.
- As a parent wanting to ensure that my children have access to everything life has to offer, I expose them to situations and do my best to provide them with lessons to keep their options open and point them in specific directions.
- As an author, I have a story I'm trying to tell or a governing philosophy I want to communicate. That idea then gets drilled down into chapters and words of my book.

Although you can wander through life like a butterfly and hope you end up well, the better course of action is to be proactive and assertive in chasing your aspirations, just as a lion chases prey. The first lesson in that methodology involves learning to define the outcome. These days I'm a lot less interested in the means to an end than I am in the end result itself. It's the outcome that first and foremost defines success at a task.

Of course, now you want to know the best, most efficient way to obtain your desired outcome. When possible, the easiest way is simple. Just do it. It is amazing how many of us turn a straight path into a crooked one by creating obstructions for ourselves. We doubt ourselves. We surround ourselves with negative people and energy. We don't come into a situation unburdened of past difficulties or failures. You must learn to focus on the opportunity, not the obstacles.

In this day and age, it's rare to stumble across an original thought. It's also rare that you'll need to. There are such things as "best practices" and "standards." If you are beginning any project attached to an outcome, it should make sense to you to invest a little bit of time and discover if what you're trying to accomplish has already been done. If it has (and it is likely that it has), you would do well to review the steps taken in the past that translated to success and see if those steps are applicable to your circumstance. If and when they are, you've just saved a lot of time and effort. For example, computer scientists sometimes incorporate another person's code into their own because that other person has come up with a good solution to a problem. Even when you're being innovative, it's very important to utilize standards and best practices as a bridge across your new path.

Even though the shortest distance between two points is a straight line, that doesn't mean the fastest way to get from one point to another is to walk there. Running, jumping, or flying between two points works even better. Learning when and how to deviate from the path is an additional skill you would benefit from having; being able to successfully deviate from the path is a true sign of expertise and efficiency.

- You can argue with the merits of presidential executive orders, but you can't argue that it's not an efficient way of streamlining the political process.
- Advanced Cardiac Life Support (ACLS) is a standard of guidelines used by health-care providers to facilitate treatment of patients at risk of death because of failure of the heart and/or lungs. It's generally best for these guidelines to be followed, but emergency physicians and cardiologists regularly opt out of these guidelines and still have great success.

Once you've identified the desired outcome of your effort, every job can be broken down into a series of individual smaller tasks that move you closer to your goal, regardless of the path eventually taken. The great thing about this realization is many of these tasks can be accomplished at any time and in almost any setting. The inefficient individual believes everything must be done in one setting and at a time specifically designated for the task.

Think about it. If you have to travel thirty miles, you can safely get to your destination in two hours if you're going fifteen miles per hour or in one hour at thirty miles per hour. However, how about getting there in thirty minutes at sixty miles per hour, assuming legality, of course? The point is, we're accustomed to the level at which we train ourselves to perform. The challenge is creating increasing levels of efficiency without adding stress or other undesirable considerations.

Let's review what we've just discussed:

1. Define the outcome.
2. Work backward to design your strategy.
3. Divide the strategy into bite–sized, easily accomplishable components.

Next, let's discuss the various levels of efficiency and apply those to implementing your strategy.

CHAPTER 3

Levels of Efficiency

Organized. Productive. Efficient. Prolific. Seemingly Timeless.

There are levels of efficiency. It's pretty important for you to be aware of this for several reasons. Not everyone can or desires to achieve every level. Some will view the energy and effort needed to become prolific as mentally fatiguing, even if I tell you that the end result includes having more available time and a happier existence. Becoming efficient certainly requires an upfront and ongoing investment in time and a fair amount of mental gymnastics to progress through various levels.

Too many of us float through life without appreciating the awesome ability we have to control our experience and destiny. We plod through our days, hoping and wishing that things will get better. We wait until the last possible moment to complete tasks, regardless of their complexity. We target dates such as New Year's to engage in self-improvement activities, instead of embracing daily opportunities. Of course, that's fine if it works for you and keeps you happy, but when asked, so many of us state we'd like to become more efficient and learn how to free up just a bit more time, either to accomplish additional things or to spend time enjoying life. As a means to that end, let's review the various levels of efficiency.

Get organized. None of what follows occurs without first becoming organized, especially with your time. Your best possible outcomes won't be achieved if you don't become goal-oriented. The outcome is what is important, not the process. It's the end, not the means, that matters. You can't be productive if you don't produce.

So many of us view becoming organized as adding more work. I'd suggest it is just a work investment that pays off by freeing up time once you figure out a system that works for you. I certainly don't know anyone who is substantially successful who isn't also impeccably organized. The bottom line here is that in order to be the most efficient and productive person you can be, it's essential that you see the value in getting organized and have the discipline to get and stay organized.

You likely are wondering about the best ways to get organized. Being organized is about developing habits. It's putting in place a system that works for you to tackle what needs to be accomplished. For at least some things, most people are organized. You have a routine in the morning between when you wake and go to work. You have a routine to prepare yourself for going to church or going on a date.

Being organized doesn't necessarily mean you have to be a micromanager. At every level, it involves setting up your system. For example, if you're a boss, it still takes an appropriate amount of organizational skill to delegate responsibility to others who will complete the minutia of some tasks for you!

The methods you use to prepare for your work tasks can serve as a template to apply to other aspects of your life. Here are some simple examples. Do you start your day looking at a daily planner or a to–do list? Do you otherwise review the items you want to prioritize? Do you maintain an ongoing list for when you go to the grocery store, or do you meander through every aisle and pick out what you think you need? Do you maintain separate piles of white and nonwhite clothes so that when it's time to do the laundry, you're already set to go? Do you maintain your receipts and financial documents in a constant place for easy access when needed?

You can and should apply organizing tactics to as many things as possible. The purpose here is not to tell you what to organize but to plant the seed that you need to get organized. Productivity breeds both more productivity and more available time. Many people are actually organized to the extent of having conducted home inventories. Sounds excessive? Well if you ever are the victim of a burglary or home fire, you'd be glad to have that inventory.

One very important consideration in being organized is you have to stop relying on your memory. You have all kinds of tools at your disposal. The vast majority of us use smartphones these days. When random thoughts or action items needing completion pop into your consciousness (but you're not in a place where you can add it to your to–do list), leave yourself a quick voice recording, or type the thought in your notes application (or other some other standard area) to be retrieved and better filed later.

Also, create redundancy in reminding yourself about things needing to be done. Alarms don't need to exist just to wake you up. They can serve as prompts to work on projects or alert you to approaching deadlines. Multiple alarms going off to remind you of an appointment is not nearly as much of an annoyance as missing an important meeting. There are many similar functions at your disposal to approximate the things an assistant might do for you.

Get productive. Actually accomplish something. There's a huge difference between activity and accomplishment. Quit shuffling those pages around your desk, and get them in your outbox. Getting organized is activity. Getting items off your list is being productive.

Of course you accomplish things. You do so every day. You manage to get out of bed. You stay gainfully employed. You maintain some level of health. You retain the love of your family. These are all outcomes, and you are doing something to accomplish and sustain these things.

Productivity speaks to meaningful accomplishment. Do you have a to–do list? Be productive, and knock some items off the list. Do you have deadlines? Readjust your activity schedule to get everything finished a week prior to the due date instead of at the last minute. Your ability to reach this level of productivity will set the table for multiple levels of success. You should make operating in this manner a priority.

However, if you really want to maximize your productivity, learn to optimize your environment. We all have people in our lives who serve various functions, formally and informally. Optimizing productivity involves matching talent with activity. An applicable saying in baseball is, "Owners own, managers manage, and players play." If your various endeavors are set up such that you can spend most of your time doing the things that you do best, you're more likely to be maximally productive. Learn to delegate those activities that can be done by others.

I mentioned earlier that I'm an emergency physician. In that field, one way in which optimization is found is in the organization of emergency departments, both in structure and assignment of responsibilities. For example, the nursing stations in well–designed emergency departments allow for a full view of and easy access to all patient rooms. Also, electronic medical records allow for more complete and easily accessed patient information.

Emergency department staff design allows for optimal productivity and efficiency (we'll discuss the efficiency aspect later on). The physicians, physician assistants, nurse practitioners, nurses, and various technicians who work in emergency rooms are all extremely skilled and talented. However, each professional is generally charged with performing a specific scope of work. When everyone focuses on his or her set of responsibilities, this allows everyone to perform at his or her highest level of productivity. For example, even though nurses have a tremendous experience base and can very quickly identify many different patient diagnoses, they wouldn't be as productive as physicians in that same capacity. Similarly, physicians would be far less productive (and efficient) if the job required us to perform the functions of technicians, doing things such as obtaining electrocardiograms (EKGs).

Next become efficient. If productivity is getting the job done, then efficiency is getting the job done in less time. From a work perspective, productivity may be the difference between keeping your job or not. In other words, it's a sign of competence. Efficiency may be the difference between barely keeping your job and getting a raise or promotion. The difference between the two is meaningful. Efficiency represents a level up on the route toward maximal effectiveness.

Of course, the question is, "What makes one efficient?" Simply put, it's the time component. Efficiency is squeezing time out of a project. That point made, there are multiple ways to be efficient.

Some people just get it. Some truly creative people, just based on a description, are able to see projects and other tasks in total. They are not only able to visualize a desired path toward the outcome but can also visualize a variety of alternative routes. Execution of the plan is almost second nature. We recognize the ability to conceptualize these alternatives as "out of the box" thinking and applaud it when it leads to efficiency.

Some people just know it. Individuals sufficiently experienced in a process are able to see the project in total simply based on a description, largely because they've already done it. They are able to visualize various paths toward the desired outcome, based on past experience that likely included trial and error as well as success and failure. Efficiency comes with knowing how to navigate the difficult road ahead. Bill Murray's line from the movie *Groundhog Day*, when he describes God, is a brilliant description of this concept. "Maybe he's not omnipotent," Murray says. "Maybe he's just been around so long he knows everything." It also explains why customers get promptly referred to senior technical-support advisors after the initial (outsourced) technical-support representatives have expended a certain amount of time with you.

Some people just know how to navigate. The concept of a well-oiled machine refers to multiple parts acting in sync, all while performing their individual roles. Your best efficiency lies in being able to work around limitations and to use the best efforts of those working with you to accomplish the greater goal. Micromanaging is never as efficient as a team effort. Consider authors. We're much more efficient and effective with the assistance of editors and publishers than we would be doing everything ourselves.

Efficiency is also created through the organization, structure, and various other components of a support system. Appropriate function follows appropriate structure. For example, the American automobile industry was famously established by Ford Motor Company's implementation of the assembly line, which revolutionized efficiency. Malls are structured to allow you to engage in all types of shopping in one location. Isn't it great to be able to park your car and shop to your heart's content, instead of having to drive all over town to find various items?

I previously noted how emergency room design promotes productivity. It also produces efficiency, allowing physicians to work faster than other staff by limiting physician activity to those actions that either are performed best or can only be performed by physicians. Similarly, an efficiency measure used by nursing staffs is the use of central heart monitoring stations that allow continuous assessment of patient vital signs in every room.

You will note that for your purposes, efficiency stands on the building blocks of being organized and productive. Just as the emergency physician combines efficiency, productivity, and competence by initially and rapidly assessing patients while stabilizing them and ruling out life-threatening conditions, you can do the same with your routine activities. If you have a series of chores that involve driving, you might choose to hold off until you can perform several tasks that occur along a certain route of travel, being sure to check off items of your list as you go. You might learn to embrace online banking activities such as bill payments, instead of going to the mailbox or standing in line at the bank or ATM to withdraw funds. Instead of going shopping and doing so haphazardly, you might choose to call the store in advance to see if they have your desired item at your desired price, or you might shop online. Some stores will pull the items you ask about and have them waiting for you! There are a million such examples. The challenge is to get you thinking about how you can arrange your activities more efficiently and to then get you acting on opportunities.

Next become prolific. Can you successfully complete multiple tasks simultaneously or in rapid succession without compromising quality? This is the art of being prolific. For some people, the thought of trying this is stress inducing. However, I would suggest this is just a function of what you've trained yourself to do. Personally, I always get a rush working in busy emergency departments. We call the art of managing a busy emergency room, complete with patients coming in and going out with seamless efficiency, "moving the room." There is a rhythm involved in simultaneously caring for one patient while doing so in a way that creates a flow for the entire emergency department. We time patient interactions based on knowledge of when labs and x-ray results are likely to come back and when medications given to patients are likely to become effective. We consider and make sure the sickest patients are able to be brought back promptly and treated effectively, while ensuring those patients who are ready to be discharged or admitted are done so promptly. All of this must occur while keeping patients and their families involved and informed. When it's going well, managing the controlled chaos of an emergency department feels like conducting an orchestra. One way to look at it is if you're going to have to care for multiple people at the same time, you probably should not only learn to get good at it but to enjoy it. The same should apply to your efforts.

One immediate question that may have come to your mind is, "Why would someone want to work on several things at once?" In many instances it's really not that you want to do this, but life often places you in these situations. Consider the parent caring for his or her young children while preparing dinner. Consider the executive overseeing various managers. Consider the air traffic controller dealing with an emergency while maintaining all the additional normal routing considerations in play. There are consequences for not becoming efficient in these circumstances.

However, being prolific isn't just about crisis management. Being prolific is another incremental step in becoming more organized, productive, and efficient. Let's skip ahead to the desired outcome. If you are prolific, you will have your choice of one of two very desirable options:

- Take advantage of the additional time you create for activities that provide you personal pleasure and enjoyment.
- Take advantage of the additional time you create to reach even greater heights and accomplish even more.

Based on what you've read thus far, it should stand to reason that you can't be prolific if you aren't impeccably organized, productive, and efficient. Being prolific is about outcomes. To be prolific is to produce large quantities of your desired outcomes. It also requires mental and (in many cases) physical stamina.

Becoming prolific is also a function of successful mental gymnastics. In most instances, prolific individuals work up to their current level of productivity by conditioning themselves to perform at this level. Success at this level requires skill in prioritizing the essential components of your activities as well as those necessary to reach the final outcome. Watching a truly prolific person is noting artistry and an expert at work. Try to appreciate the efficiency of those in charge if you ever spend time in an air traffic control tower, in a producer's booth or watching a crowd being controlled. Don't just marvel at the efficiency. Recognize that these are levels of performance we all can and should strive to achieve.

Finally, there's being seemingly timeless in your productivity.

Do you know people who are just always doing something—and not just "doing" something but getting something accomplished? With enough conditioning and practice; being organized, productive, and prolific might not be just a habit but can even become your calling card, from the time you jump out of bed in the morning until you fall into bed at night. If this sounds hectic to you, trust me, you're missing out on a lot of fun! This is how you "change the world!"

What is most interesting about super efficient individuals is not that they appear hyperactive or otherwise abnormal, but their understanding that achieving this level of proficiency is simply the result of hard work that becomes incrementally easier. Your brain can accommodate more than you're currently challenging it to perform. Developing it to become better organized and more efficient is within your reach.

The consideration of being super efficient isn't limited to your personal productivity. Most successful business owners enjoy the benefit that a well-designed, well–honed operational infrastructure brings. In this example, once the infrastructure is set up correctly, it works for you without your direct involvement. In business, that's called "making money in your sleep."

There's always another level. You can continue to add layers to your proficiency. You can become more organized. Within your organization, be it a corporation or your personal endeavor, you can attain greater productivity by delegating responsibility so others around you are taking some of the load off of you and performing at their individual maximal levels of productivity for your benefit. The key here is to embrace the challenge and internalize it so it becomes fun. Your quest for efficiency should be viewed as pleasurable instead of tedious. The quest for self-improvement will change all aspects of your life. Embrace it. Put in the work.

CHAPTER 4

Eliminating Time Suckers, a.k.a. Efficiency Killers

repeat it time and again. Time is your most important asset. Ultimately, where and how you spend your time is the ultimate referendum on your priorities and values. If you are wasting away your time on frivolous activities, that's fine if that works for you. Just realize that your actions reflect your life choices. For example, in choosing to read this book, you're trying to become more productive. Let's continue the conversation.

Addition by subtraction is a real thing, especially when it comes to productivity and efficiency. As you become more and more productive, you will come to appreciate the value of your time. You'll likely become less tolerant of wasting time with irrelevant activities when you know you could be participating in meaningful activities or spending quality time with family and friends.

There are time suckers all around you in the form of people, activities, and responsibilities.

- Many of us already know or have intuitively figured out that a thirty–minute TV program has about twenty-one minutes of programming and nine minutes of commercials. That means you could be about 30 percent more efficient in your TV watching if you record the program, watch it later, and skip the commercials. Alternatively, you could be about 70 percent more efficient if it's the commercials you really wanted to see. Of course, it must be said you could save 100 percent of your valuable time in avoiding "boob–tube" components of television watching. Have you ever thought about just how much TV you watch for no reason at all when other more meaningful and stimulating options exist?
- Speaking of television, if you like to watch sports, have you ever noticed a good game gets your heart racing? Have you considered taking advantage of that adrenaline rush and walking a treadmill or otherwise exercising while you're watching sports? Instead of being a couch potato, use your sports-watching activity to your advantage!
- Have you ever heard that the typical American spends two years of his or her life waiting in line? Knowing this, why wouldn't you learn when the more efficient times are to go to places like the bank, the department of motor vehicles, the grocery store, and the post office? Can you adjust when and how you go to work to avoid traffic jams?

- How much of yourself do you give to people and conversations when you know the relationship or talk isn't going anywhere, all the while knowing you have something really important to do or somewhere else you need to be? If this sounds like you, you've valued courtesy above your own interests. That may make you a nice person, but it makes you a nice person who isn't going to be very productive as long as you're allowing yourself to be imposed upon.
- Just how much time do you spend on social media? Do you use it as a means to an end or as an alternate reality? It is not hard to imagine that you can spend the entire day on various forms of social media, all the while sucking away any productivity you could have had. Imagine what could be accomplished if you actually were working while at work or were using social media to advance your career instead of just chatting with your social media acquaintances.

You want to eliminate efficiency killers. Fortunately, it really doesn't take much more than setting priorities, being consistent in focusing on those priorities, and being assertive in your pursuit of them. Invest a bit of time up front in respecting your priorities, and you can alter your life forever.

A great way to start this process is to engage in a period of quiet reflection and introspection into your life. Make an honest assessment about your activities and direction. Are you heading down a path that you'd like to maintain and advance? If not, are you really powerless to make a course correction? Does your relative lack of accomplishment result from a lack of power, organization, or motivation? You have to find whatever is within you that will allow you to better direct your energy and effort toward what will make you happy and productive.

Here's another fundamental consideration. If you have an interest in being productive, let alone prolific, you need to take care of your mental and physical health. A sound body really does enhance a sound mind. If you don't have healthy eating habits and a regimen of physical fitness, you haven't made an honest enough commitment to achieving your highest possible level of productivity.

Similarly, you must decide to eliminate toxic environments from your life and those items that bring negativity into your life and reinforce it. These are productivity killers. Focus on surrounding yourself with the support you need to be your best and to perform your best. Drama in your life is a dish served somewhere else, unless you're an actor.

Learn to say "No" and mean it. Learn to be definitive in your decisions, and learn to make better choices. Too many of us are beholden to bad decisions simply because of the seeming lack of other options. I always tell people when they're being guilted into doing something they know is not in their own best interests, or they neither have the time nor desire to do, to take a few deep breaths, gather your thoughts, and in the most respectful way possible, just say no. A bad idea at a good time is still a bad idea. When you make a decision to make a change, you can't be afraid for it to be abrupt. There's no reason success has to occur incrementally. Need to quit smoking? The majority of those who quit successfully do so by quitting cold turkey. Need to remove yourself from an abusive relationship? As soon as you have a plan that will allow you to do so safely, leave. It's not a debate: removing yourself from a toxic environment means you'll spend less time being unhappy and more time being productive and advancing the rest of your life.

Learn to say "Not now" and mean it. A good idea at a bad time is a bad idea. You will perform better if you continuously prioritize your activities and focus on the issues of highest priority. Just because something else presents another option or crisis doesn't mean that it automatically assumes the place of highest priority on your to-do list. Doing this requires diligence on your part to actually think about both the task at hand and which of the options in front of you actually represents an opportunity worth pursuing.

Perhaps at this point you're thinking, "When do I get idle time to refresh and recharge?" That's a different conversation, and we'll discuss that later. Before you start thinking about relaxing, become productive enough so you can have the time to fully enjoy your well-earned breaks.

CHAPTER 5

Mastering Multitasking—
Training Yourself to Be Efficient

ave you ever wanted to be a juggler? Odds are that you already are. Each of us bears the burden of multiple responsibilities, yet many of us pretend that our activities have to be linear, focused on one thing at a time. The early points here are twofold:

- If you're going to have to do something, you might as well learn to become good at it.
- Your brain will accommodate your activities if you train it to do so.

Perhaps you're worried about the stress of having too much on your plate. That's fair. I'm not advocating you overextend yourself, but you should learn to better manage the items already on your plate. You'll pardon me if in time you discover that you become better able to do more than you're currently able to do! Besides, the best way to address having too much on your plate is to remove some of it (preferably through completion of the tasks). Learning to do this is certainly better than choosing to stress out over it.

Frankly, I always laugh when I hear so–called experts saying we aren't able to effectively multitask. My response to them: you aren't doing it right! It may be true that you can't be in more than one place in a time or have more than one actual thought in any given instant, but it certainly is the case that we can effectively manage more than one task at a time. For starters, multitasking is simply applying a higher level of organizational skills to everything you need to accomplish. We've already addressed some of the essential components you need to be a great multitasker.

- You must be organized and focused. You can't expect to do well juggling several tasks if you're haphazard in your approach. You won't do well if you get easily distracted from the tasks at hand or wait until the last minute.
- You must be efficient. You may be surprised to learn that most of what you are actually doing while multitasking is discovering the ability to address similar components of several tasks at the same time. For example, you may already have the habit of paying your bills online at the same time or going shopping for yourself and others.

Usually, I spend most of the day multitasking. I really don't even think of what I'm doing as multitasking (or even work for that matter). I just get tasks done. In addition to any efficiency you achieve in batching similar aspects of different tasks, multitasking works because your brain performs better when you take a break from any given activity. Sometimes instead of taking a break, you can simply switch between tasks and keep on going. Perhaps you've heard of state-dependent learning, in which you learn and recall better in certain environments. This phenomenon is similar to that, and I describe it as "state-dependent fatigue." The cure to it is switching gears. This represents a more productive way of incorporating positive distractions into your routine. Instead of allowing new items to interfere with the task at hand, place them in the rotation and get to them when you need a change of pace.

If you really enjoy what you're doing, multitasking feels like a form of play. I've been a physician for over twenty years, and when I step outside of the immediacy of the moment and reflect on what I'm actually doing (e.g., caring for more than five patients at a time), I find it part wonderful, amazing, and hilarious that people allow me to do the things I do. I bring this up to say if you can develop a similar mindset about your work, you'll be better at it, less stressed, and more able to build upon your work and eventually multitask. Of course, you must commit to making good choices about the challenges you accept, and you must have a sufficient level of productivity.

"But what about the mental fatigue?" First of all, if you become fatigued, take a break. Learning to multitask is learning to condition your brain. You don't start training for a triathlon by running one on the first day, do you? Learn to push the envelope on your abilities. Commit to continue working until you're no longer being productive or are no longer enjoying yourself.

A final point: not every chore can be part of a multitasking session, particularly in the early stages of your development. You don't want to compromise the quality of your work by not paying it the attention it requires. You will learn in time when you're proficient enough to handle multiple tasks, and you will be able to identify which tasks have a level of complexity that require you to give them exclusive focus and time. Remember, even the juggler learned the skill with only two balls in the air at first.

With these considerations in mind, here is a series of principles that will keep you effective and moving forward while multitasking, instead of creating more clutter in your life:

- Have clear goals, a plan of action, and a plan of attack.
- Keep your goals, action plans, and to–do lists accessible and visible.
- Even when you're multitasking, prioritize your activities based on importance and deadlines.
- Reduce your goals into items small enough to complete quickly so that it wouldn't be disastrous if you got interrupted while working.
- Be focused.
- Alternate between tasks if and when you need a break.
- Take a break when you need a break. A fresh brain performs better.
- Connect your tasks so you can efficiently bundle some of them while working.
- Perform the fun and creative tasks first and the mundane, relatively mindless tasks later in your work session.
- Be mindful of your performance. You're conditioning your brain. Learn to identify and act on opportunities for improvement.

CHAPTER 6

Blinking to Higher Levels of Efficiency

The next two chapters represent especially advanced levels of proficiency. This is where you want to be when you are a really high performer. If you've never heard of "blinking" or an implementation matrix, get ready to not only learn them, but I'd suggest you make the terms a part of your everyday vocabulary.

However, let's first pick up from a few concepts that were previously mentioned. Having a level of proficiency so advanced that you're seemingly timeless in your productivity is akin to what professional athletes call being in "the zone." Now being in the zone is not some kind of magic; I want you to view it the way golfers do. They sometimes refer to this so–called luck by saying, "The better you are, the luckier you are." The point here is your expertise creates desirable outcomes, even when you seemingly make mistakes. All the levels of productivity and activities that have been mentioned up to this point work to develop a productivity instinct so sensitive that you're intuitively performing without having to make the conscious decision to do so. At this level, you've developed your brain and organized your routine and activities such that efficiency seems to occur effortlessly, as in the blink of an eye. It is at this point that you'll really be able to perform a higher volume of activity over the course of your day. You'll also note an ability to complete a higher complexity of activity with the same effort that it previously took to finish simpler tasks.

You should neither take the blinking process for granted nor believe this will replace the work needed to perform. Blinking simply represents an enhanced level of performance. To obtain the level of performance you seek, you still need to put in the work and get organized, and you still need to maintain and build upon your levels of productivity and efficiency.

Any of you high performers already know this to be the case. There are times when you're challenged with an issue, and you instinctively know what to do next. This phenomenon was described at length in the Malcolm Gladwell book *Blink: The Power of Thinking Without Thinking*, but these abilities have been around much longer than that.

The entire specialty of emergency medicine involves the phenomenon of "blinking." Here are a few examples of how it works.

- Recognition of critical diseases based on visual, verbal, and other (often minimal) sensory clues is often a matter of life, limb, and death. Emergency physicians often make "picture diagnoses" just on the basis of a patient's appearance and the visual clues offered.

- Knowledge of what next steps are needed in critical cases, and when drastic measures are appropriate instead of conservative treatment, is an essential and advanced skill. Whether the threat in question is a heart attack, stroke, diabetic coma, or an amputated body part, emergency physicians appreciate that "time is tissue," and being able to kick–start ("blink") into gear is not the same as treating patients after performing a prolonged history examination and physical examination.

- Practicing emergency medicine in a busy emergency room is basically the same as practicing disaster medicine. When there's a volume of five or more ill patients presenting at a time, emergency physicians don't have the luxury of only addressing one person at a time. As a patient, you'd go nuts waiting, and even worse, critically ill patients may suffer horrible consequences while waiting. The ability to "move the room" describes the efficiency process of not only caring for multiple patients simultaneously but also being able to prioritize interactions with those patients based on their medical needs. It also includes addressing the desire to move patients expeditiously through the system. There is a lot of "blink" involved in this process.

This same process occurs in many high-powered, high–pressure jobs and activities outside of the emergency room. Whether you're a gym teacher herding a large group of children, a policeman managing a riot, or any of many other professionals, what's applicable to you is the following: as you become more and more efficient, pay attention to your increasing ability to engage in making correct decisions rapidly. That ability means you're performing with high productivity.

CHAPTER 7

Living with an
Implementation Matrix

"Blinking" doesn't allow you to live your life as if "the Force is with you." When you're performing at this high a level, you'll need a complimentary level of organization to accompany your new skills. If you've never heard of an implementation matrix, I'd suggest you pay close attention and learn to add (at least) one to your repertoire.

I've always been of the mindset that tasks are best removed from your plate at the earliest opportunity. At any given point in time, I have so many activities that I'm performing that I don't have time to remember to do something later. I'd rather get it off my plate as soon as possible, as long as it doesn't interfere with a higher priority or time-limited item on my list. That's why I'm accessible. Let's get it done and move on to the next challenge. I generally don't have time for patience.

I live my life on the matrix. Not in *The Matrix*. That was a movie, and it wasn't real (or was it?). Once you become organized, productive, and proficient, and you're comfortable as a multitasker, your ongoing efforts will be aided by developing a personal organization template so in sync with you that it cultivates and propels your success forward.

An overly simplistic way of understanding an implementation matrix is to think of a project plan that you separately apply to each of your significant activities. In fact, implementation matrices are meant to also display ongoing progress on any endeavor. I've used project plans for years as a health-care consultant, and they work wonderfully to keep you organized, keep your team accountable, and keep you on schedule.

The basic idea is to identify whatever outcomes you seek; identify the specific, individual actions that will produce that outcome; and assign a timeframe for completion. For your personal implementation matrix, it is essential to list every single item of importance. You want to reduce your actions to every step along the way (every bite of the proverbial elephant you need to digest). I'd challenge you to whittle your tasks all the way down to those that can be implemented in five minutes (this is an aspiration, not a requirement). If you're completing an organizational matrix, you will also include notations about who is responsible for each of the actions needing completion. In either circumstance, it will be helpful to set target dates for completion.

Let's get this established up front: this doesn't work until and unless you've mastered the earlier levels of productivity. Having a matrix in front of you will be very frustrating until you're very organized, productive, and efficient. Establishing a matrix will require an initial investment of time. You will need to think through the process. You will need to define what objectives you seek. You will need to determine the best means to those ends. You will need to break down the components required to complete each step along the way. You will need to establish timeframes for all of this. Furthermore, if you are developing an organizational matrix, you will need to assign tasks to everyone involved in the process. All of this necessarily occurs before you actually begin doing the work.

The implementation matrix also allows for tracking progress. If it helps, listing percentages of the task completed allows you to know where you are along the way. Alternatively, a simpler system, such as denoting red for "not started" or "no progress," yellow for "some progress," and green for "completed and operational" accomplishes the same end.

Having an implementation matrix dramatically simplifies your life. If you think through the process and objectify the tasks before you start the work, your stress level will be much lower than it would be otherwise. I remember watching my wife plan our wedding. She was so organized that by the month before the blessed event, all that was left to do was pay the bills (and of course the wedding went off grandly).

I have always enjoyed utilizing an implementation matrix with my employees. I consider it truth serum, a reflection of just how well-organized my team is on a project and in general. When you're managing very large projects and delegating tasks to people, or even allowing administrative assistants to manage part of your life, you need to be confident that their level of organization will get the job done for you.

The matrix can be as extensive as your life gets. That shouldn't mean it gets more complicated, but as you add projects, it does become more detailed. If you're getting a picture of you becoming beholden to a massive spreadsheet with charts and graphs, that really shouldn't be the case. You'll discover that you're "blinking" through many of the items on your list during your workday, and you're referring back to your matrix to make sure you've stayed on course.

The implementation matrix is best complimented with a to-do list. As items pop into your consciousness, you have the choice of either addressing them immediately and being done with them or adding them to your to-do list. Maintaining a to-do list addresses a very simple problem many of us have. At some point during the day, we invariably will come across idle time. It's important to note I'm not referencing any time you have allotted for breaks or pleasure; I'm referring to times during the course of the day when you've perhaps finished one task, you need a break from your current task, or you're just not able to address your preferred task. For example, maybe you're on an airplane for a few hours or maybe you have a stretch between meetings. This would be a great time to review your to-do list and knock off a few easily accomplishable tasks.

The only difficulty with the matrix is figuring out how to organize it and execute its components. We'll get to the execution part a little later. However, I will say now that I consider the philosophy behind using implementation matrices to be the answer to another misguided concept: growing pains. I refer to growing pains as "a reflection of inadequate organization." Wal-Mart Stores, Inc. and Apple manage tens of billions of dollars annually, and I doubt they're sitting around complaining about their rate of growth.

The *72 Hours in a Day Workbook* includes samples of implementation matrices. Play around with these and learn how to develop your own. Your ability to use an implementation matrix and further your efficiency just gets better with time and practice.

CHAPTER 8

Five-Minute Efficiency

n the context of what we've been discussing, allow me to reassert some barriers and opportunities. To be as organized as you need to be, you'll need to identify the many tasks and components that make up a project. To be as productive as you need to be, you'll need to learn to tackle projects, regardless of the size. To be as efficient as you need to be, you'll need to learn to work within tight timeframes and not necessarily be limited to only doing your best when you have dedicated time. To be as proficient as you need to be, you'll learn to avoid considering an excellent effort a not completed project because it's not yet "perfect."

Obtaining the best efficiency level won't occur in one fell swoop; your efficiency is measured by the sum total of all the different activities you do over the course of your day. You can complete each project or task you have by carrying out a series of small actions. It's a skill to be able to visualize a task and see it both as a series of parts and the sum of those parts. However, many of us only see projects as big challenges, and we often feel better able to work on these when we are in the frame of mind to "meet the challenge" and complete them in one sitting. Many of us tend to avoid our work altogether until we feel sufficiently motivated. This should sound familiar to anyone with an inclination to procrastinate on a job or cram for a test.

Imagine if you had the ability to view and attack a project in increments. Surely there are always some components of projects that are easier than others. There may be times when you're up to working on the most challenging parts of your various projects, and there may be other times when you're not. During these times, there are probably enough minor components for you to work on so you could stay productive. Working toward this end guides you to the concept of five-minute efficiency.

Five-Minute Efficiency challenges you to perform in two ways.

- Learn to think of your projects as a series of small, connected projects. Seek to break your activities into the smallest possible tasks, so much so that these tasks can be completed in as little as five minutes.
- Learn to become so efficient that you can accomplish the task you're working on within five minutes. You can do this either by breaking down your tasks into smaller components or by becoming more efficient at addressing the task at hand.

If you are a taskmaster, you'll find five-minute efficiency a better approach to obtaining productivity from others. As you start working with implementation matrices or just giving out assignments, seek to break down the larger projects. Of course, some tasks may require maximal effort due to its complexity, but there will also be simpler tasks that are easy to complete. As you time the completion of projects, perhaps you could seek to switch between harder and lesser tasks. By doing so, you'll give your team a rest from the complex tasks while maintaining the momentum caused by continually getting things done. You'll find this approach breaks any monotony work may bring and generates satisfaction within the workforce. However, to fully apply the concept of five-minute efficiency, the skilled taskmaster will learn to break the tasks down to as many of the simpler tasks as possible, so much so that the entire project continues humming along without the starts and stops that complex tasks are likely to bring

If you are simply trying to stay efficient, you will find your days much more productive if you're staying active. Even when you don't feel up to tackling the toughest items on your list, you can stay productive and get things done. If you're really good at breaking the bigger tasks into smaller pieces, you may even discover that you actually have eaten the elephant one bite at a time!

I refer you to the *72 Hours in a Day Workbook* for examples of using Five-Minute Efficiency. Remember, this is an aspirational goal. Celebrate your improvements in efficiency instead of stressing out over an inability to reach the ultimate target.

SECTION II

Applying Efficiency throughout Your Life

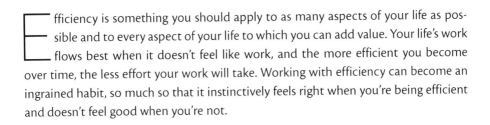 fficiency is something you should apply to as many aspects of your life as pos-
sible and to every aspect of your life to which you can add value. Your life's work
flows best when it doesn't feel like work, and the more efficient you become
over time, the less effort your work will take. Working with efficiency can become an
ingrained habit, so much so that it instinctively feels right when you're being efficient
and doesn't feel good when you're not.

CHAPTER 9

Efficiency in Organizations

As physicians in training at a county hospital, we learned to perform just about every nonadministrative function in the hospital. The notion that we really could do it all was actually tested when a nursing strike occurred. This method of preparedness is not the ideal organizational structure, but it is nice for purposes of testing backup capacity. Unfortunately (or not, depending on your point of view), many organizations have taken to "redesigning" staffing patterns to shoehorn many employees into performing multiple jobs as a routine course of action. Having nurses serve as the cleanup crew, or having physicians perform clerical staff functions may create short–term financial savings but could end up costing organizations in the long-term. Employee satisfaction and perceived desirability as a place to work could decrease, and organizations might even experience financial losses.

In the normal course of operations, physicians don't take on the role of jack-of-all-trades in the clinical setting. Nurses, technicians, and all other members of the team make specific contributions that often cut across formal job descriptions and work toward helping patients. In emergency medicine we like to say, "Cheating is good." Among other things, this refers to the notion that any effort or any information from any source that works to the benefit of the patient is a good thing. Of course, in the middle of a patient resuscitation, the physician is at the head of the bed and his or her voice is the one everyone listens to. Still, organizational structure and function have components of both rigidity and flexibility that can contribute to operational efficiency.

Among the many different emergency room staffing design models, the highest level of organizational efficiency occurs when physicians are given the space to think. In fact, it is the level at which a physician is able to think critically about patient care that differentiates physician specialists from everyone else in health care. Evaluation of potential diagnoses, life threats, and treatment needs (especially for critical patients) is more a science than an art, but it requires appropriate use of both the scientific and creative mind. Also, considering the mental fatigue that occurs over the course of the day, keeping the brain fresh not only optimizes performance, but it also optimizes efficiency.

Organizational structure not only affects how organizations function, but also determines the ability of the individuals within it to do their best work. The way an organization is structured should reflect and build upon the mission, goals, and operations of that entity. That structure will determine the level of production and satisfaction of employees and/or team members. Organizational structure necessarily creates a feedback loop that propels the entity forward or leaves it stuck in the mud. When ideally structured, it leaves those working within it feeling free to grow the organization beyond its obvious goals. When it's poorly structured, staff members often put in minimal work.

Although this book focuses on personal performance, there are important lessons to be learned from the structure and function of organizations. These lessons are applicable to how you perform in your own personal and professional environments.

You should be aware of the two types of organizational structures. Horizontal (a.k.a. "flat") organizations encourage an open process, encouraging everybody with a stake in the organization to offer input in the development and execution of its mission, goals, and methods. Team roles are still well-defined, but the method of organizational operations is flexible and permits dialogue. Vertical (a.k.a. "tall") organizations are more authoritative in structure. Those in leadership roles set goals and directions. Team members are expected to complete tasks to accomplish these goals, but they aren't given much opportunity for input or feedback.

You may be able to conceptualize the circumstances in which each model may be preferred. If you're developing widgets, a vertical structure may be best. If the goal is to simply produce a predetermined quota of product, the unique skills of employees don't matter as much as their collective ability to deliver the desired end result. Alternatively, if your task is related to innovation or problem solving, a horizontal structure is likely to get to a good result. After all, it doesn't matter where a great idea comes from; it's still a great idea. In many instances, you'll find yourself in a system that uses components of both structures. Employee feedback is often welcomed and encouraged to a point. Many organizations encourage employee contributions by using such contributions as a component of the employee evaluation process.

Regardless of the organizational structure, there are a few components of organizational behavior that represent peak performance and efficiency, such as the following:

- Better performing organizations clearly communicate mission, values, desired goals, and expected outcomes. They find ways to maintain a motivated workforce. They promote an air of ethics and fairness within the workplace in assignment of work, evaluation of performance, and promotions.
- They have contributors who operate at their optimal level of performance, doing what they do best and performing what those with a lesser degree of skill can't do. They are deliberate in placing team members in positions that match and utilize their best skills.
- They allow a sufficient amount of input from their contributors so that contributors feel some level of ownership over the final products and outcomes of the organization. They maintain a sense of connectivity between units of the organization.
- They respect your time instead of wasting it. Highly efficient meetings gatherings for actions instead of passive lectures.

Each of these considerations has some degree of applicability to your personal interactions and methods of conducting your work. Actively look for how efficiencies you have achieved in one aspect of your life can be applied to other areas. This next chapter addresses those considerations.

CHAPTER 10

Efficiency in Work

At any given point in time, I'm literally working with a few hundred individuals. It's a head-scratcher to see some people wander aimlessly between tasks, performing them only when things pop into their heads and/or at the last minute when they're up against a deadline. It's no wonder job satisfaction levels are so low for so many.

We want to feel good about what we do and want to believe we can be proficient in accomplishing our work. Sometimes work environments are such that many employees are without incentives to accomplish more than is required of them. In these instances employees believe that displaying a certain level of competence and productivity will mean being given additional work than being rewarded.

I'm reminded of a consulting job I had in the Washington, DC, area. The vendor's scope of work allowed for four years to accomplish the task. I determined the work could be accomplished in eleven months. Would you believe the response I got? It was something akin to "Slow down. In DC, we're used to doing things like the government. We like to work in increments of four years." Given I'm more interested in accomplishment than activity, we went ahead and got it done anyway. We only have this one life to live, and I'd prefer not to waste time. It's my most valuable asset.

Let's discuss ways that work activities can be made more productive. Of course, there are a wide variety of activities that are more or less applicable depending on whether you're an owner, manager, or employee. The goal here is to identify opportunities that will make your individual work environment more productive. As mentioned in the last chapter, there is some applicability in the methods of highly productive organizations that will serve you well.

Highly efficient workers are organized and focused. They clearly receive and understand directions. They systematically address and complete projects. They use their time during the day on the work at hand without allowing all manner of other distractions to diminish the quality or amount of their output.

Highly efficient workers are motivated. Whether self-motivated or incentivized, workers who deliver their best efforts invariably have bought into the mission and goals of the effort. This level of ownership of the process will further compel peak performance from other team members.

Highly efficient workers use resources. They tap into tools and ask others for advice when needed. They are better able to be efficient because their resources and networks support their activities.

Highly efficient workers are flexible. Part of being organized involves knowing which resources should be used to achieve the desired goal. Some jobs require a sledgehammer and others require a chisel. It's best to know how to use these different tools and when is the appropriate time for each.

Highly effective workers appropriately seek guidance and feedback when needed and have the capability to be autonomous when appropriate. They incorporate feedback and tailor activities to the specifications of a project. They exhibit a thirst for additional training that improves their performance and skill set.

Each of us has managed to carve out a segment of our lives in which we serve a role as a leader. We also have other segments of our lives in which we serve as an assistant to something greater than ourselves. Be mindful to treat those working with you or under you with sufficient respect so as to create an enjoyable atmosphere. Treat others the way you would like to be treated. The way you interact matters, and it makes a difference.

CHAPTER 11

Efficiency in Health

Your life's work is not limited to your time at work. Your activities involving the other aspects of your life are likely equally or even more important to you, and thus it becomes even more important to develop efficiencies. I can't think of a better place to start than a discussion about your health.

This shouldn't be that difficult to understand. Poor physical and mental health are rate-limiting factors in your pursuit of efficiency. If you have mental or physical disabilities, that fundamentally limits some of what you can perform. In many instances, physical and mental limitations alter the priorities in your life such that the focus needed for peak performance necessarily won't be there. On the other hand, good physical and mental health are templates upon which you can maximize your productivity. Appreciate that you must survive before you can flourish. You can't lead your most productive life if you're spending an excessive amount of time in an emergency room.

Have you noticed how energetic and productive you feel when you're physically healthy and without stress? Are you able to jump out of bed during the day, feeling encouraged to get started? You should hope so. Your morning brain offers you the best chance to get certain tasks done. The healing process that occurs during a good night's sleep should have you primed to be productive throughout your day.

These considerations address the "why" of good health. Your issue is the "how" of efficient health. Let's review key components of both physical and mental health. Acquiring good health is so much easier than we make it appear to be. In fact, it is very impressive how poorly we attend to our physical and mental health. When it comes to good health, there's no app. You must put in the work and command the discipline necessary to protect and maintain your health. There are some simple principles that will get you to where you want to be.

Physical health is about discipline. This discipline is exhibited by prevention and maintenance. The single most efficient thing you can do for your health is to not get sick. This sounds so simple, doesn't it? However, in practice we continue to demonstrate how difficult it is.

Your diet fuels your body. Everything you place in your mouth either incrementally helps you or harms you. In medicine we generally assume your diet is about 75 percent of the health battle. It is the height of health efficiency simply to fuel your body with nutritious substances. There are no magic potions or pills, and you're better off without the fad diets. If you're motivated to begin any diet today, try one that includes plenty of fluids and a plate filled with dark green vegetables. That's a good start.

Specifically taking the time to know about the Healthy Eating Plate, as constructed by the Harvard School of Public Health, would add an important tool to your arsenal. Here are some of the key components:

- Fill half of your plate with produce (fruits and vegetables). The broader the variety, the better. Sorry, but potatoes and french fries don't count as vegetables!
- Fill a quarter of your plate with whole grains. Whole grain foods help lower the risk of coronary heart disease, stroke, obesity, and diabetes. The sure way to know you're choosing a whole grain food is simply in the name. When you're grocery shopping, the product will actually say "whole grain." This is not the same as multigrain.
- Fill the rest of your plate with a healthy source of protein such as fish, poultry, beans, or nuts.
- Use healthy oils—such as olive and canola—when cooking, on salad, and at the table. Avoid butter and fatty salad dressings.
- Regarding beverages, do yourself a favor. Try to drink water, and rediscover how refreshing it is. You don't have to pay for another beverage just because you're used to doing so. Tea and coffee are healthy options if you use little or no sugar. Milk and other dairy products should be limited to one to two servings a day.

Of course, most of us are not absolutists and do things "in moderation." The pursuit of a healthy diet means migrating toward the ideals mentioned above until you've incorporated these principles as your new normal. You may have also noticed the absence of desserts in the Healthy Eating Plate. You should consider desserts a reward or special treat, not a staple of your meals. If you're eating more than four desserts a month, you're less health-efficient than you are if you're eating less than this.

Exercise assists our physical health. There are so many layers to exercise, but health efficiency requires drilling down to the actions that produce direct, measurable outcomes.

Remember that your heart is a muscle, the purpose of which is to pump blood with its nutrients and oxygen around the body, supplying your organs with fuel. The more efficiently that muscle performs, the healthier you'll be, because your vital organs will stay nourished. It's important to restate that everything is relative, so starting with most any regular activity that's more than your current baseline will improve your conditioning and eventually your health.

Consider these demonstrated benefits of exercise:

- Exercise controls your weight by burning calories.
- Exercise reduces your risk of cardiovascular disease by improving your heart's function. It lowers the risk of both heart attacks and strokes.
- Exercise reduces your risk for type 2 diabetes and combinations of high cholesterol, high blood pressure, and high glucose levels (together known as metabolic syndrome).
- Exercise specifically reduces your risk of colon and breast cancers, and it probably reduces your risk of endometrial and lung cancers.
- Exercise improves the functioning of your immune system.
- Exercise strengthens your bones and muscles, and it keeps your joints functioning well.
- Exercise maintains your mobility and agility, improves your ability to perform the activities of daily living, and prevents falls as you age.
- Exercise slows the development of arthritis.

It should be easy to understand that it's much easier and more efficient to invest the time exercising than to have to struggle with any of these diseases on the back end.

The next exercise issue to address is how much exercise is actually needed. You need aerobic exercise that increases your heart rate for at least twenty to thirty minutes at a time for three to five sessions per week. Learn your target heart rate for your age, and exercise to get into that range. If you exercise regularly, your metabolism will better approximate that of a fine-tuned machine rather than a sputtering old car.

Healthy diet and exercise also combine to help you have and maintain a good metabolism. Here are five tips to raise your metabolism, which is close to the very definition of health efficiency.

1. **Eat smaller meals, and eat more frequently.** It's true. More meals more often are better, but only if they're smaller. Calorie counting is still a major part of the equation. The point of more frequent meals is to prevent the body from going into starvation mode, which slows your metabolism as the body attempts to conserve energy. If you do this, you'll discover those meals are smaller and you will get closer to eating more appropriate portions than we typically do. Also, make those in-between meals healthy choices like a handful of fruits or nuts.

2. **Prime your pump.** Remember, it's all about your heart's ability to efficiently move blood around the body. The healthier your heart is, the better your metabolism will be. You need aerobic exercise that increases your heart rate for twenty to thirty minutes at a time. Learn your target heart rate for your age, and exercise to get into that range. Your metabolism will better approximate that of a fine-tuned machine rather than a sputtering old car.

3. **Weight train.** This is very simple. The more muscular you are, the more calories you will burn, especially relative to someone of the same weight who is obese. Not only will you become a finer calorie-burning machine, but also, in this case, you actually will look better! Add weight training to your exercise regimen.

4. **Choose the fish (and not the fried variety).** Fish oil contains substances called omega-3 fatty acids (EPA, DHA). These substances increase levels of fat-burning enzymes and decrease levels of fat-storing enzymes. Daily ingestion has been shown to help by metabolizing away an approximate four hundred additional calories a day.

5. **Enlist a personal trainer.** Everyone needs help and motivation. Some of us need a lot of help and a lot of motivation. We also need expertise. There's nothing more frustrating than working hard yet not seeing any results because you're working incorrectly. A good trainer can put you on the right path, supervise your regimen, and hold your hand through the process. A good trainer can manage the minutiae of age, sex, and body habitus considerations that also play a role in this. Your ideal trainer will have knowledge of nutrition, wellness, and supplements that are tailored to your specific considerations. This will get your metabolism revved up!

It is important to discuss the role of toxins in affecting your health efficiency. We've already noted the role of diet in delivering toxins to your body, but our other habits directly affect our health and ability to live an efficient life. Be advised: your body is constantly under attack, both from our environment and the things we do to ourselves.

The skin is the body's largest organ and suffers from injuries caused by the sun, microorganisms, and trauma. Avoidance of these threats and utilization of simple measures of moisturizing (e.g., drinking plenty of water and other healthy fluids and using lotions and moisturizers) goes a long way toward maintaining skin health.

Toxicity to the heart and brain comes in many forms, but you should be most concerned about the blockage of arteries, which heavily contributes to heart attacks and strokes. The diet, exercise, and stress-relief measures discussed here will reduce your risks for these diseases. Early recognition is important for giving you the best opportunity for a good recovery. Here again, the theme is the same. Prevention is better than cure.

Toxicity to the lungs occurs from more than cigarette and cigar smoke, but cutting smoking out of your life is the most efficient way to cut your risk of lung disease. Just consider the action of delivering black smoke and a myriad of additional toxins into a clear space meant to deliver oxygen to the bloodstream to fuel your body. When discussing the lungs, you must also be mindful of infection prevention. Why don't more people wear masks when loved ones are suffering from pneumonia or the flu? Protect yourself!

Toxicity to the kidney and liver should concern you. When you discover there are substances that completely damage and overwhelm the organs specifically meant to detoxify us, that should serve as a serious warning about what could happen next, and we would do well to minimize our exposure to such agents. Alcohol abuse, illicit drug abuse, and certain combinations of prescribed medications are especially frequent causes of kidney and liver toxicity, as is the deterioration of general health. Kidney disease frequently results from high blood pressure and diabetes, which is why when these diseases are uncontrolled, a slippery slope awaits.

Substandard mental health brings its own challenges, but the end result is the same as it is with substandard physical health. Needing to cope with depression, schizophrenia, or other mental illnesses precludes one from focusing all of his or her time productively. Being able to perform at one's best involves both the addition of positive influences and the removal of negative influences that are known to lead to or have resulted in behavior disorders.

We can objectify the conversation and identify what is most likely to make you unhappy and lead to depression. You may or may not find this hard to believe, but outside of medical causes of psychiatric illness and factors outside of your control, there are really three choices we make that most commonly adversely affect our happiness and mental health. Take it for what you will, but the data is what it is. Stay away from these circumstances, and you're less likely to be unhappy. Sometimes it's about addition by subtraction.

Health Problems: People who are sick or have significant illness in their families generally aren't happy. Although this may seem obvious and perhaps unfair, given that some illnesses and conditions are inherited or occur haphazardly, be mindful of the things you can control. Of course, this gets to the negative effects of obesity and smoking. More so than any other health-related activities and conditions, these will eventually lead to deteriorating health and subsequent unhappiness.

Job Problems: You don't have enough to do with your time? Yep, an idle mind is the devil's workshop, as the saying goes. It should be pointed out that neither too much work nor the wrong type of work (e.g., a job with low satisfaction) seems to promote happiness. On average, people change careers seven times during their lifetimes. These changes often occur due to a search for happiness. It's good to change jobs if that means avoiding being stuck in a bad situation. Follow the job you love, and you're more likely to be both happy and successful.

Relationship Problems: You make bad relationship choices? Well there's one specific choice that is shown to be most likely to reduce your happiness—choosing a neurotic partner. What's neurotic? For one particularly disruptive example, think about the so-called Drama Queens/Kings. Neurotic partners respond emotionally to events that wouldn't affect most people, and their reactions tend to be more intense than normal. They're more likely to interpret minor frustrations as hopelessly difficult. Their negative emotional reactions persist for unusually long periods of time. In short, if you want to be really unhappy, become attached to such a person. This person will negatively affect your world, keeping you embroiled in drama and unhappiness, no matter how good the financial, physical, or other parts of your relationship.

A good mental frame of mind has many positive effects on your health. A sense of enthusiasm and hopefulness, as well as the ability to engage in life and face life's stresses with emotional balance, appears to reduce the risk of coronary heart disease. Children with a positive outlook and an ability to focus on a task at age seven are in better health with fewer illnesses thirty years later than children with a negative outlook. Optimism cuts the risk of coronary heart disease in half.

It isn't that hard to be optimistic. It just requires a rewiring of some of our outlook on life. Make a change today. Become a more positive person, and you'll become a healthier person!

Try these examples:

- It's true. The glass is half-full. It's your choice whether to view that way or as half empty.
- You always have something upon which you can build. If you focus on and accentuate the positive in your life, it will define your existence.
- Positive is as positive does. Whether or not you believe in karma, there's a joy to be found in being a positive force in the world. You'll feel good about yourself if you find yourself doing good for others.
- Place yourself in positive environments, and you'll find yourself feeling more positive. If your friends and circumstances are wallowing in negativity, at some point you can't help but be dragged down in the dumps. Compel yourself to make friends with sunnier dispositions, and seek out environments in which positivity flourishes.

Considering the above, incorporate these specific mental lifestyle changes, and reap the benefits:

- Seek to have emotional vitality: a sense of enthusiasm, hopefulness, and engagement.
- Have optimism: the perspective that good things will happen and that one's actions account for the good things that occur in life.

- Surround yourself with a supportive network of family and friends.
- Have good "self-regulation," (i.e., the ability to bounce back from stressful challenges and know that things will eventually look up again).
- Engage in healthy behaviors such as exercising and eating well.
- Avoid risky behaviors such as unsafe sex, drinking alcohol to excess, and regular overeating.

Finally, there are a series of routine health measures that are essential in maintaining good health. It is understandable and unfortunate that some have bad health as a result of conditions acquired at birth or otherwise out of their control, but beyond that bad health is far too often the result of avoidable circumstances.

- Get immunizations! The value of immunizations may be debatable to some individuals, but the medical and public health literature could not be clearer. Immunizations save lives.
- Go to your physician for routine checkups and health screenings! Knowing your health is optimized will provide you the confidence to live your best life. Whether obtaining a clean bill of health or early identification and treatment of conditions, this will give you the best chance of maintaining a normal life and normal function. It probably is not a coincidence that women get yearly examinations at a much higher frequency than men, and they have a higher life expectancy.
- Take measures to prevent injury, accident, and disease. Wear a safety belt; put toddlers in car seats; use condoms; childproof your home; install smoke detectors and home-alarm systems. These are all steps that have a direct effect on your health and consequently on your ability to live a productive life.

We've reviewed a lot in this section. You might even refer to this chapter as "unlocking the secrets of health." Between having a healthy diet, engaging in regular appropriate exercise, reducing your exposure to toxins, following routine health maintenance recommendations, limiting risky behaviors, reducing your stress by eliminating negative influences within your environment, and surrounding yourself with positivity, you've set the table for a life lived without interference from debilitation. If you're doing these things, you are ready for peak productivity. Go for it.

CHAPTER 12

Efficiency in Finances

t has been said many times that money is the root of all evil. I'm not so sure. There are a lot of good people with a lot of money who make a lot of good things happen. It's been my experience that both the absence of money and the pursuit of money are much greater contributors to evil than money's mere existence. If I were correct about that theory, you would do well to become more efficient in making money and better at keeping it.

When it comes to making money, it would help to have a certain level of understanding about money. There are various ways to make money; I call them different levels of financial achievement. Ranking these levels is based on two considerations: the financial gain and any restriction the method of obtaining income places on your time.

- You have no meaningful income and are dependent on others to provide you with what you have and/or need.
- You have a salary that fixes the amount of money you can make. This amount of money may or may not be sufficient to meet your needs.
  - Jobs or careers with a higher salary reflect a higher level of financial accomplishment.
  - The assumption is salaried positions are generally very restrictive on your time.
- You have a job that pays a certain amount per hour, which may or may not be sufficient to meet your needs.
  - Being able to work additional hours to obtain additional income allows for a higher level of financial achievement.
  - Financial considerations being equivalent, the more desirable job will be the one that is less labor intensive, permitting the opportunity to multitask.
  - You have a contract or other situation that provides you a certain amount of money per hour or other time unit. In this situation, others provide the work on your behalf.
    - This is the most desirable situation from a financial efficiency standpoint, as it places the least restraints on your time given that you can hire individuals to perform almost every aspect of the contract, and you are left to collect profit. Because you have not squandered much time in this scenario, you are free to repeat the situation with

as many additional contracts as you can obtain. This situation is known as "making money in your sleep." When you make money in other ways—such as from the interest you make off your savings account, retirement accounts, or other investments—they say "your money is working for you instead of you working for your money."

As you review the above considerations, you will notice the progression from having no meaningful finances to being employed (either in a job that pays per hour or that is salaried) to being a business owner with passive income streams. The main financial efficiency consideration in this progression is that at some point, you cash in your time for financial gain. For most, the goal is simply to do so for as much money as possible, but for the entrepreneur, the goal is to retain as much time as possible.

At some point in your personal and business lives, incremental time is more important than incremental money. With a labor-intensive job, you cash in your ability to do anything else. When your job environment offers you the efficiency equivalent of seventy-two hours in a day, you can repeat your moneymaking endeavors again and again. When your efficiency level has reached near-timelessness, and you're making money in your sleep, the actual number of hours in a day really places no limit on to what you can accomplish. It is true in business as well as in your personal existence: optimal function follows optimal structure. The extent of your being organized determines the ceiling of your productivity.

In the above discussion, you notice another key to financial efficiency: the successful pursuit of passive revenue streams. It should just make sense (and certainly feels good) to make money without ongoing physical work. Everyone would do well to have residual checks showing up in their mailbox. That is what maintaining free (i.e., available) time does. Free time is more important than time spent (per hour) working for money because each increment of free time allows you to continue to pursue more money.

An additional consideration for your pursuit of money and financial independence is what I call "being on Fifth Avenue." If you have done well in protecting your time and in generating passive revenue streams, at some point you can create at least five separate and independent revenue streams. Maybe you have a job. Perhaps you also own real estate that generates additional income. You may be a partner in a small business or two. Some of you sit on boards that offer salaries for participation.

The obvious benefits of being on Fifth Avenue are twofold. Of course, you'd like to have more money. Additionally, having multiple revenues streams provides you with a lot of insulation. Imagine if you lose your main source of employment or any of your other revenue streams. Being on Fifth Avenue will largely allow you to keep on keeping on, and it will reduce the financial blow taken by losing income. Contrast this with only having one job and losing it. This is often catastrophic. We often hear about diversifying our savings portfolio. Diversifying our income portfolio is just as important!

The idea of being on Fifth Avenue isn't just to have different revenue streams. It provides you with indefinite options to become more and more efficient. You shouldn't just pursue five revenue streams. In time you'll want to pursue five revenue streams that are incrementally closer to the highest level of financial achievement. When you can go from one job to five jobs to five sources of passive income, you have truly achieved financial efficiency on the income portion of the financial equation. Of course, there is no magic to the number five. You can replicate the process as many times as you like.

Now, about digesting that elephant. Truly addressing the challenges of minimizing expenses and maximizing savings seems like such a colossal task for so many. Whether you are a millionaire or struggling to get by, whether you're single or part of a family of four, there's always another level of financial achievement. Money is to be respected in any denomination. I know plenty of affluent individuals who swear by the adage "Pennies add up." If you're frugal or prudent with your pennies, they become dollars, then tens of dollars, and so on. Eventually, you'll find yourself in a position to reap the rewards or other desired benefits of cutting costs, spending less, and saving more.

However, "Pennies add up" isn't a plan; it's a philosophy. You need to take the time to develop a personal financial plan. Your journey of a thousand steps should begin with a plan, not a first step. Are you able to develop a plan? You likely know some of what you want. Try objectifying the conversation with your loved one or business partners. (Presumably, if you're in business, you're operating under a business plan, but I'm not making assumptions here.)

No matter the specifics of your personal financial plan, there are certain tried and true principals that will apply. Achieving these principals represents financial productivity. Optimizing your use of these principles is where efficiencies occur. In other words, there are situations in which one principle may be more applicable that another. As a reminder, without productivity, there is no efficiency.

- **Develop the plan within your plan.** Operating without a budget is like flying without an instruction manual. If you're not planning to get anywhere, odds are you'll get nowhere. The habit many have of spending until the money runs out is not the smartest course of action. Take the time to identity your actual needs. Adjust your life to accommodate those needs. Make sure your actual needs are contained within your actual income.
- **Pay yourself first.** For many, this is the toughest hurdle to cross. So many people live paycheck to paycheck. That is often because they don't properly identify their actual needs. When you complete your budget, you should protect yourself from both short- and long-term shortfalls. Establishing a habit of putting aside 10 to 20 percent of your income (at whatever your level of income is) allows you to protect yourself from life's unfortunate pitfalls and secures your long-term financial security. Teach your children to begin this habit as early as possible.
- **Protect yourself.** You accomplish this via the forecasting that occurs with budgeting, and you do so by paying yourself first.
  - You also protect your financial health with insurance. As frustrating as it is to seemingly shovel large amounts of money to auto, life, and health insurance companies for mishaps that never seem to occur, it is nothing less than devastating to be wiped out financially by an unexpected illness or accident.
  - Protecting yourself also should include maintaining an emergency fund of two to three months of your income in the event you become disabled or otherwise lose your income.
  - Another important component to protecting yourself financially is not allowing yourself to fall behind on your taxes. This is a slippery slope from which recovery can seem to have no end.
  - Finally, when it comes to your money, you would do well to work with a financial advisor who will help you sort through all of the above options. You will make a lot of money over the course of your life. The sooner you

learn how to use it and get advice from professionals, the better your performance will be over the long haul.

Once you have a plan, you want to put that plan into action. Wherever you are on the various levels of financial achievement, you want to get the greatest possible level of efficiency from your money. We've discussed income generation; however, wealth is not just about revenue generation. Sometimes the best offense is a great defense.

You already do this on your own, maybe without realizing it. You clip coupons. You turn down the heat and air conditioning in your home, especially when you're away. You shop sales. Maybe you buy in bulk quantities. These and a thousand other tips that represent living frugally are means to an end. I trust you to be creative enough to discover these opportunities as they present themselves. It is much more important for you to really understand sound financial principles.

An important principle that will help you practice financial efficiency is incrementalism. Picking up on the theme of "Pennies add up," be aware that every dollar you spend paying your debts matters. Have you ever paid attention to the interest rates you pay on your bills or receive on your investments? The sooner you pay off your debts, the less money you'll lose.

Here are some actions for you to take.

- Create a list or spreadsheet of all of your bills, including your mortgage or rent, credit card bills, automobile payment, and so on.
- Rank those bills by the interest you're paying.
- This rank now represents your priorities for paying bills.

If you're committed to paying your bills early or having additional money to pay beyond the amount due with each payment, you should first attack the bill with the highest interest rate, regardless of the amount owed. Then you will systematically work down the list based on the highest remaining interest rate. Many people like to pay bills off in total, but with regards to financial efficiency, that's the wrong decision. You will save yourself more money by paying down a loan of any type with a 10 percent interest rate than paying off a smaller loan with an interest rate of 8 percent.

There is an important caveat to this consideration. Any financial decision you make that has taxable consequences needs to have a higher priority than routine decisions. Your cumulative tax burden is such that this point will almost always apply, and this applies whether you're paying bills or saving money. This is the main consideration behind why you are encouraged to save money in retirement funds. For example, if you're in a 30 percent tax bracket, the most financially efficient decision you can make will be to maximize your contributions to all available tax-deferred savings plans. In this same example, one hundred dollars of pretax savings represents a 30 percent more efficient use of your money that just saving one hundred dollars without any interest accumulating.

There's no time like the present to make these changes. Quit hoping and wishing for financial success, and start working on your plan. There's always a reason why it seems like you can't begin a project, but you must learn to focus on the opportunities, not the obstacles. An excuse is a tool for fools, used to build bridges to nowhere and monuments to no one. If you're driving down the financial road of life without a bridge, the crash won't be pleasant. You hold the keys to your financial future.

CHAPTER 13

Efficiency in Recreation and Pleasure

'm sure when it comes time to enjoy yourself, being efficient isn't the first or second thing to come to mind. What does one have to do with the other? Why stress over efficiency when you're trying to have a good time? For some things, the enjoyment is partially found in not having to rush, right? Those last questions may make a lot of sense until you find yourself stuck in traffic going to a sporting event or standing in line for what seems like forever at an amusement park.

No matter the event, you have options and choices, and you should always be aware of where efficiencies lie. There are two components to consider in maximizing efficiency when it's time to relax. One is the decision of what you want to do, and the other involves the logistics of how to do what you've decided to do. Allow me to remind you that efficiency is getting more done in less time. Who doesn't want to have more fun and actually be able to perform more of his or her own most desired activities than before? For those of you that embrace spontaneity as part of the fun, just be sure to balance that with an understanding that spontaneity hits a roadblock when you have to wait for long periods of time to engage in your desired activity. If these situations can be avoided with just a bit of prior planning, it doesn't have to spoil the magic in the moment found with being spontaneous.

The decision about how you choose to spend your time off is the old "quality time" consideration. Although some of us enjoy relaxation and quiet time, others enjoy making memories. I'd suggest these don't have to be mutually exclusive! There's a time for spontaneity, but when people make bucket lists during their golden years, they tend to get very specific, don't they? There's a way to plan your fun. Recreational fantasies and dreams are best thought of as plans to be put in action.

Why not take the time to list the recreational items you'd like to accomplish now? Put them on your radar. Part of the enjoyment of an event is the planning and anticipation of it. The efficiency is found in this fact: the more you do and the more you accomplish, the more the world opens up to you, and the more you're subsequently able to accomplish. Just as when you're filling a jar with rocks and sand, you get more in when you place the rocks as a priority and fill in sand around them. Planning some of your fun doesn't take away from your ability to fill in the gaps with spontaneous activity; you'll do that anyway based on opportunities that present themselves. Just make sure you don't miss out on your big-ticket items.

The logistics of making your recreational dreams come true make the difference between your recreational time being everything you wanted it to be or a headache that wasn't worth the trouble. Prior planning permits peak performance. If your wedding day, trip of a lifetime, first date, or girls' night out ends up as the culmination of a well-planned episode, you will likely have a better time than if the planning was shoddy or if there was no planning. No matter how tedious it seems to plan an event, if it comes off as planned, you will deem it as having been worth the effort.

Think about what you're doing. It's that simple. If you take the time to get organized, your event will be more enjoyable.

- Does the timing of the event matter? If not, save yourself some headaches and plan it away from peak hours. You'll likely be able to save time and money without compromising quality. If timing does matter, can you plan your activities so everything flows smoothly and is efficient?
- Are there specific components that will make the event more enjoyable? People have a general idea about must-see or must-do activities during an event. Highlighting these activities and planning around them gives you a great starting point for organizing.
- Is the event a big enough an affair that it requires an implementation matrix? Have you heard people who organize parties and other events comment that it seems that everyone ends up having more fun than the organizer? It really doesn't have to be that way. If your planning is sufficient, your event will enable you to truly be a host instead of a worker. This will result in more enjoyment for everyone, particularly if you're the one your guests were actually coming to see. Have your event sufficiently planned so you can spend the event enjoying the fruits of your labor.

Now go have fun, and make planning your event part of the fun.

CHAPTER 14

Efficiency in Relationships

Simply put, relationship efficiency is all about improving communication.

- Ladies, how much time have you spent thinking, "Will he, or won't he?"
- Men, how often have you wondered, "What exactly is she thinking?"
- At work, do you find yourself working under unclear instructions?
- At home, do you feel like you're speaking a different language than your kids?

In a world of billions, let's not pretend there aren't an untold number of different types of relationships. Much time is wasted in assuming that individuals are operating under the same mores, standards, and practices. You'll accomplish much more in a relationship from the beginning if you're open and able to communicate about expectations and goals.

I am fond of pointing out that it's not fair to demand outcomes if you haven't set expectations. This is applicable to all manner of relationships, including family, dating, and business relationships.

Consider these points:

- Take the time to discuss what you want and need.
- Take the time to discuss what's unacceptable, intolerable, and criteria for terminating the relationship.

As much as we'd like to believe it to be the case, it's a recipe for disaster to just believe your employees are competent. You may end up quite disappointed if you blindly trust that your partner in a relationship is compatible just because an attraction exists. There is work involved to get relationships to where you want them to be.

Many of us are more comfortable "leaving well enough alone" and not knowing the facts than being forced to make hard decisions, particularly if there's the risk of upsetting your personal apple cart. That's a choice in itself. From an efficiency standpoint, having your eyes and mouth wide open is the best way to get to wherever it is you want to be in your various personal and business relationships.

When it comes to relationships, "straight, no chaser" isn't a style made for everyone. Being the proverbial bull in the china cabinet that is a relationship isn't often the best course of action. Some people are very sensitive and fragile. Others are brittle, and still others are easily agitated. Learning the sensitivities of those in various relationships with you is an efficient relationship tactic. Once you know those sensitivities, you'll likely do a better job of navigating the relationships.

It's never really all about you, even if you've been made to feel that way or believe that it is. If you act like it's all about you, you run the risk of chasing away everyone in your life. Once again, communication is the best way to learn where the minefields are in your developing relationships. Take the time to learn the rules and enjoy the benefits of making the right decisions.

SECTION III

Benefiting From Efficiency

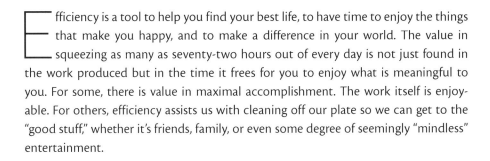fficiency is a tool to help you find your best life, to have time to enjoy the things that make you happy, and to make a difference in your world. The value in squeezing as many as seventy-two hours out of every day is not just found in the work produced but in the time it frees for you to enjoy what is meaningful to you. For some, there is value in maximal accomplishment. The work itself is enjoyable. For others, efficiency assists us with cleaning off our plate so we can get to the "good stuff," whether it's friends, family, or even some degree of seemingly "mindless" entertainment.

CHAPTER 15

Discovering the Value of Seconds

'm always telling people that my time is my most valuable commodity. As you get older and life becomes busier, the demands on your time can become enormous. You literally can never have enough time at home with your family. You need to spend a (usually) defined amount of time at work. There are priorities you'd like to get around to addressing that involve your personal aspirations and things you just like to do for yourself.

The decisions you make about how you spend your time become a reflection of your values and your priorities. Are you a good father and a dedicated husband? Are you a trusted employee? Are you a valued member of your community and/or congregation? Are you a fanatic sports fan? There really is not enough time in the day to be everything that you could possibly be.

You discover that you have to make choices. You'll make choices that prioritize the various parts of your life. Sometimes you'll do this consciously, and sometimes you'll make the statement of priorities without knowing it. When you're squeezed for time and you decide to simplify your life by putting something off or removing something from your life, sometimes you are glad that you've eliminated waste from your life. On other occasions, you wish you had more time to enjoy all the things that are meaningful and/or available to you.

That's why seconds matter. Just as pennies add up to dollars, seconds add up to valuable time than can be spent on the activity of your choice. The more efficient you become, the more time you will have available for all those meaningful options.

This is why being organized is so critical. Organization is the base upon which productivity and efficiency stand. If you're disorganized, you spend much of your day not only figuring out what to do but also how to do it. Your progression through various levels of productivity makes all manners of things possible. Instead of focusing on obstacles, you focus on opportunities. Instead of feeling stress, you feel excited about challenges. Instead of viewing your life's work as, well, work, it becomes a form of play—just like you envisioned it when you were a bright-eyed child, saying this is what you wanted to do when you grew up.

Being organized and proficient to the extent of near-timelessness advances your abilities to increase productivity, both by removing waste and by adding positive activity. It really involves thinking about and prioritizing where your time should be spent, making choices that allow you to stay on that path, and being consistent in executing your plans. It's realizing that every option is not an opportunity. If you're truly efficient, every opportunity shouldn't be an option. By the time you're prolific enough to achieve as much as you desire, your happiness really won't be a question, and you'll relish the realization that there is value in every second of the day.

CHAPTER 16

It's All about Execution

Typically, those involved in teaching efficiency would be telling you to document what it is you do with your time as an initial step. I don't need to ask you to document your activities over the course of a day to demonstrate if you are or aren't efficient. You already have a sense of whether you're doing a good job of accomplishing all you need to do or hope to do. However, wherever you are in the progression, you can become more efficient. There's always another level. You will get there with a progressively deeper understanding and application of the principles of efficiency.

We've already discussed the levels of performance at length. We've also discussed how efficiency frees up your time. In my example, I've performed hundreds of jobs across the country for a wide variety of clients as a consultant. I don't usually get contracted because I know more information than anyone else. Ask any employee at your workplace how he or she feels about consultants. They'll invariably tell you they know exactly what to do if someone would just listen to them or give them a chance. I get contracted because I'm an expert at implementation. I take ideas and make them reality. Remember, productivity and efficiency are based on outcomes, not just creative brilliance.

The difference accounting for my relative degree of success and the really important consideration for you is that it's not enough just to know what you're supposed to do. Achieving outcomes involves knowing how to get the job done. Navigating the shark-infested waters of your work or personal life is not easily accomplishable. The problem is your approach to productivity. Completing tasks when you get around to them or when you remember to do them is neither the sign of superior organizational skills nor a formula for efficiency. Implementation of a plan is the final and most important step in productivity. It's always about reaching the end result. The means taken are much less important.

As far as it relates to your personal productivity, the name of the game is practice. If you are really interested in being more productive, you will accept that this is an active process. You will need to become diligent in seeking opportunities to create efficiencies. The route to becoming prolific and even timeless in your activities involves a lot of mental exercise until your actions seem as if they have become second nature.

Some parts of this process are much easier than others. Recall that you're making actual decisions to eliminate activities that are wasteful, time-consuming, or that otherwise don't represent your priorities. Some of these activities will involve individuals or other current commitments. As noted, early and honest communication will go a long way to clearing away any stress these situations are contributing to your life.

You will have to accept the angst that comes with creative tension. Many tasks are not performed efficiently or at all because we are not willing to break the proverbial eggs needed to make an omelet. Your actions and activities demonstrate your priorities. If you are really interested in accomplishing your tasks, sometimes the most efficient route involves placing pressure on yourself or others to rise to the challenge and to perform to your expectations. Accepting less than others' best often means accepting less than your desired outcome. Weigh your options, define your outcomes of interest, make your plan, and implement it without being deterred. That's efficiency in action.

Ultimately, you are "the message," whether you realize it or not. You either are inspiring and motivating to those around you, or you're not. This is fine if your goal is simply to go along to get along, but if you're interested in your most productive life, a big part of that will be the effect you have on others and your ability to connect to and associate with those who will assist you in your efforts. Having a track record of productivity and a persona of being organized and effective will open a lot more doors for you than may otherwise be the case. Be the message.

CHAPTER 17

The Gains of Your Efficiency: Application Equals a Better Life

ifferent friends either tell me I always seem to be working, or I'm never working. They tell me I'm always working on something, or I'm always accessible. The funny thing is all of those comments are probably true. I'm usually working when I'm relaxing, and I'm definitely relaxing when I'm working. How is this possible? When you enjoy what you do, it just doesn't seem like work.

What they're actually saying is I'm accomplishing a lot. I'm nowhere near a workaholic. Every work task I take is a means to an end, an effort to secure the future, and a design to build something meaningful. If you felt your work was meaningful and more enjoyable than the alternative of just working at a task without having or appreciating a bigger picture, isn't it logical that you'd want to spend more time doing it?

See, I'm for time off as much as the next guy, but my question to you is what exactly are you accomplishing with your idle time? Just because your time is idle doesn't mean it can't be meaningful. What exactly is idle time? Is it time with your family? Is it time enjoying your favorite pastime, such as a sporting event or a spa day? Even something like spending time chatting with or consoling your friends can be meaningful. Nothing about these types of activities is idle. We would do better to describe these as activities that aren't related to work. Again, we work to live; we don't live to work.

Of course, you get to choose how to spend your time away from work. Whether you decide to sit around and watch television, spend your time on social media, or volunteer at a soup kitchen, that's your decision. Once you've been productive enough (whatever that means to you), your valuable time becomes your own. So why not get there as quickly as possible?

Activity is not the same as accomplishment. Productivity equals accomplishment.

I'm not suggesting that you should rush through life or spend every waking moment trying to work. Certainly, a big part of life's joy is found in its quiet moments. This book's goal is to demonstrate that virtually every aspect of your life can be made more productive and lived more efficiently. Incorporate this knowledge into making your life happier and more meaningful. This quest of ours is about productivity, not more work.

If and when you get to the point to where you're productive enough to claim there are seventy-two hours in a day, I'm certain you'll be thrilled to have discovered it. There is a vibrancy found in treasuring every second and acting on your seconds as if they're meaningful. It is empowering to spend your days making active decisions about where and with whom you spend your time. This vibrancy is the reward of efficiency, and trust me: it's well worth pursuing. Enjoy the journey.

About the Author

Jeffrey Emery Sterling, MD, MPH

D r. Jeffrey Sterling is an international leader in community-based medicine and health care.

- He serves as president and CEO of SterlingMedicalAdvice.com, an international public health initiative providing personal and immediate healthcare information, advice and telemedicine to consumers, businesses, corporations and governments.
- Dr. Sterling also is president and CEO of Sterling Initiatives (SI), a healthcare consulting and implementation firm assisting entities with clinical, operational, and financial best practices. SI has assisted health systems, health plans, state governments, and medical practices in three-dozen states and

countries. SI has gained particular notoriety for its work in creating "centers of excellence" among hospitals and other healthcare entities. Dr. Sterling is also author of the healthcare blog "Straight, No Chaser" at www.jeffreysterlingmd.com.

- Dr. Sterling also is president and CEO of SI-STEMS, an emergency medicine contract medical group that provides staffing and management services to hospital across the United States.

Additionally,

- Dr. Sterling serves as president of the Northwestern University Black Alumni Association, representing approximately 5,000 alumni nationally organized in twenty-six local chapters.
- Dr. Sterling has served as CEO, senior VP, corporate medical officer, national physician practice director, and regional medical director for various health-care contract management groups, and as medical director for seventeen emergency medical system units and home health companies.
  - Dr. Sterling has served as chairman and/or medical director of the departments of emergency medicine at the following level I trauma emergency departments: John Peter Smith Health Network (JPS) in Fort Worth, TX
  - Prince George's Hospital Center, Cheverly, MD (Metro DC)
  - St. Joseph Regional Medical Center, Milwaukee, WI
- Dr. Sterling founded DFW Urgent Care, a series of award-winning urgent care centers in Texas, New York, and California providing quality equivalent, cost-effective care alternatives to hospital emergency rooms.
- Dr. Sterling founded the Minority Association of Pre- Health Students (MAPS), a national organization of premedical and other health career aspirants with chapters in over 300 colleges nationally.
- Dr. Sterling served as the founding medical director for JPS Health Network's Sexual Assault Nurse Examiner (SANE) program and created the first SANE program in the state of Connecticut at Connecticut Children's Medical Center.
- Dr. Sterling founded DS Comprehensive Psychological Consulting, a contract management firm providing optimization of care for those in need of acute behavioral intervention, working throughout New Mexico and Texas.

- Dr. Sterling founded US Asthma Care, a series of outcomes-based, best-practice disease management treatment facilities in Texas and Illinois working with health plans to reduce hospitalization and improve clinical outcomes among asthmatics.
- Dr. Sterling founded and served as medical director of the Covenant Healthcare Asthma Clinics in Milwaukee, then the largest asthma education clinic in Wisconsin.
- Dr. Sterling has served on the board of the Asthma & Allergy Foundation of America, Texas Chapter, and the American Lung Association, Central States Region.
- Dr. Sterling served as chairman of the DFW Minority Business Council's Health Industry Group, a consortium of over seventy healthcare business enterprises across the Dallas-Fort Worth Metroplex.

Dr. Sterling has degrees from Northwestern University, Harvard University School of Public Health (health policy management), and the University of Illinois College of Medicine, and he completed his emergency medicine residency at Cook County Hospital in Chicago.

Dr. Sterling is a speaker in high demand on topics of asthma, pneumonia, acute coronary syndromes, healthcare economics and healthcare disparities, having delivered over one thousand lectures nationally.

Made in the USA
San Bernardino, CA
17 April 2017